The Settling of the Manor of Tara
A dual language edition

Translated by Morgan Daimler

ISBN: 9798519024945
Imprint: Independently published

Introduction

This work is the second in a series of full translations I have done of well-known Irish myths. The original Irish is from the manuscript col. 740 published by RI Best in Ériu vol 4, 1910, used with permission; the English text is entirely my own as are any and all errors within. As I have been given permission to use the middle Irish text this book, unlike my previous work the Cath Maige Tuired, will alternate between Irish and English verses; I hope this will help give readers a fuller view of both the original language and flow of the manuscript. As with my previous works my approach favours a more literal translation rather than one which is pleasing to an English speaker's ear (or eye as the case may be). While this can make the text feel a bit stilted in English I think its important to preserve the feel of the original as much as possible rather than edit to fit a different audience.

Although heavily Christianised this myth nonetheless offers fascinating insight into older beliefs including references to the various mythical groups which settled Ireland before the arrival of humans. The

Insertion of Christian elements and situation of the narrative within a Biblical time frame is consistent with the approach of scribes at the time who sought to provide context for their audience within the cosmology of Christianity and to place the Irish myths within a frame that referenced classical connections which were seen as validating and prestigious.

Do Suidigud Tellach Temra

1. BÁTAR húi Néill fecht and i mMaig Breg i n-imaccalaim in-aimsir Diarmata meic Fergusa Cerbaill, ocus ba hed imráidset: ba mór leo do thír aurland Temrach .i. maigen i mbátar secht radairc for cech leath, ocus imráidset a himdibe ina faithchi sin iarum. Ar ba dímáin leo in cutruma sin do fherond occaib cen tech cen trebad fair, ocus cen fhognam tellaich Temrach. Ar ba héigen dóib faichill fuilainhg fer nÉirend ocus a mbiad co cend secht láa ocus secht n-aidchi i cind teora mblíadna béos. Ba shamlaid iarum téigthea dond fleith la Diarmait mac Cerbaill. Ni théiged rí cen rígain ná ségaind cen banshégaind ná féndid cen il-íaraind ná midlach cen drúithsig ná brígiu cen bantuilc ná gilla cen lennait ná hingen cen lendán ná duine cen dán.

The Settling of the Household of Tara

1 One time the O'Neill's were at Mag Breg in council in the time of Dairmat son of Fergus Cerbail and they were discussing this: that great was the open land around Tara, that is a plain of seven views on every

side, and they discussed curtailing the green that was there. It was unprofitable to them the proportion of land there without houses or ploughing in them, and without families rendering service to Tara. There was a compulsion on them of maintaining the men of Ireland and to feed them all for seven days and seven nights in every third year. It was like this then that they used to go to the feast of Dairmuid mac Cerbal. No king went without a queen, no champion without a consort[1], no warrior without many weapons[2], no unarmed man[3] without a mistress, no hospitaller without a wife, no youth without a sweetheart or maiden without a beloved[4], or person without a skill.

---

[1] Benshegaind, literally woman-champion but generally understood as the consort of a champion, or a distinguished lady

[2] Il-iarand, unclear but I am assuming il, many multiple and iarand, weapons or armour

[3] Midlach, generally understood as a person who cannot bear weapons but by implication a coward or weakling

[4] This line 'no youth without a sweetheart or maiden without a beloved' uses two forms of the word lennán (lennait and lendán) which means lover, sweetheart, beloved (and so on). Since the text gives two forms of the word I am choosing to offer two synonyms here but I want to be clear the same word is used in the original text for both.

2. Nochóraigdis and ind ríg ocus ind ollamain im Diarmait mac Cerbaill .i. na ríg ocus na hollamain aróen, na fianna ocus na díbercae immalle. In gillanraid ocus ind ingenrad ocus int áes báeth borrfadach isna himdadhaib im na doirse, ocus doratad a chuit chóir do cechóen díb .i. mínmesraid ocus daim ocus tuircc ocus tinni do ríghaib ocus do ollamnaib ocus do sruithib slánaib sochenélachaib fer nÉrend olchena, rechtairi ocus banrechtairi ic roind ocus ic dáil dóib side. Feóil derg dano do beraib íaraind ocus fírbrocóit ocus núa corma ocus assen do fiandaib ocus díbergachaib, ocus druith ocus deogbairi ic roind ocus ic dáil dóib. Cend-chossach and dano ocus imchosail cecha hindile do aradhaib ocus do oblóraib ocus da drabarslúag ocus da dáescordáinib, ocus araid dano ocus oblóre ocus dorrsaidi oc roind ocus dáil dóib. Feóil láeg and dano ocus úan ocus orcc ocus in sechtmad dál riamid an-echtair do gillanraid ocus do ingenraid dáig nosoerfeted a medar eated ocus nobíd a n-ortán ica n-idnaidi. Sóeramais ocus banamais ic roind ocus ic dáil dóib.

2 The kings and the chief poets[5] were set around Dairmat mac Cerbal, that is the kings and the chief poets together, the warriors and the reavers together. The youths and the maidens and the high-spirited irresponsible[6] people in the cubicles around the doors and his correct portion was given to each one, that is choice-fruit and cow and boar and steel[7] for kings and chief poets and for the esteemed perfect nobility[8] of the men of Ireland additionally, stewards and stewardesses among them dividing it and among them serving it for them. Red meat from iron spits and fresh bragget[9] and new ale and milk-water for the warriors and reavers, and jesters and cupbearers among them dividing it and among them serving them. Head-legged[10] and the rest and a

---

[5] Ollam – the highest rank of poet

[6] Báeth – a legal class of people who are considered incapacitated on mental grounds

[7] Tinni is a bit tricky here; everything previously listed is food but tinni can mean anything from a rod of metal, ingot, steel, or any type of metal

[8] Slánaib sochenélachaib literally noble nobility, but as slánaib can also mean perfect I've gone with that to avoid the redundancy in english

[9] Bragget is a kind of drink made of ale and mead together. Fír may mean fresh, genuine, but can also mean milk.

[10] Cenn-chossach is an obscure term with no clear meaning. Cenn is usually given as head. Cossach means legged or relating to legs

portion of each cow and charioteers and base poets and rabble and charioteers also and base poets and doorkeepers among them dividing it and serving them. Veal also and lamb and pork and the seventh portion outside to the youths and to the maidens because their mirth used to entertain them and their nobility would redeem them. Hirelings and female hirelings among them dividing it and among them serving it to them.

3. Rohirfúacrad iarum for maithib Érend tíachtain dochum na fleidi do thig Themra co Diarmaid mac Cerbaill. Et roráidset nád caithfitis feis Temra co rochindtea dóib suidigud tellaig Temra, indus robói rempo ocus nobiad ina ndiaig co bráth. ocus roráidset re Diarmaid an aithisc hí sin. ocus adrubairt Diarmait riu-seom nárbo chóir a rád fris tellach Temra do chomroind cen chomairle fri Cendfáelad mac Scandláin meic Fingin .i. cend Érind ocus comarba Pátraig nó re Fíachraig mac na druinigi. Ettha úadib-seom iarum for cend Fíachrach meic Colmáin meic Eogain ocus dobreth chucu dia cobair, a robdar úaite a n-éolaig, ocus robdar ile a n-anéolaich, ocus robdar ili a n-imarbága, ocus robdar imdae a cesta.

3 Afterward the nobles of Ireland were commanded to come to the feast of the house of Tara by Dairmat mac Cerbaill. And they said they would not enjoy the feast[11] until the arranging of the household of Tara was decided, how it was before their time and how it would be from then until the end[12]. And Dairmat said it was not fitting to ask him of the household of Tara's partitioning without the counsel of Cendfaelad[13] son of Scandlain son of Fingin, that is head of Ireland and successor of Patrick or of Fiachra son of the embroideress. Messengers went then to fetch Fiachra son of Colman son of Eogan and he gave help to them, (because) few were their wise men, and many were their ignorant men, and many were their contentions, and many their troubles[14].

---

[11] Previously fled has been used for feast in the text. Here we find feis used, which can also mean feast but has additional connotations of a festival or extended event.

[12] bráth, literally Judgement or doomsday.

[13] Cendfaelad, literally 'wolf-head'

[14] Cesta, a form of ceist, literally questions which may work here but also with a more general sense of problems or difficulties

4. Dorocht chucu iarum Fíachra, ocus adbertadar ris a cétna .i. tellach Temra do chomroind dóib, ocus atbert friu ná bérad breth forsin caingin sin dóib co ndechasta húaithib ar cend neich bid éolchu ocus bid síne andás. 'Ca hairm a fuil sidi,' arsiad?

'Ní ansa,' arse. '.i. Cenfáelad mac Ailella meic Muiredaich meic Eogain meic Néill, is asa chind side,' for sé, 'do comgned a hinchind dermait i cath Muigi Rath .i. conid cumain leis cach ní rochúala do senchas hÉrend o shin alle cosinndiu. Is cóir cid hé thí do bar nh-ethergléod,' olse.

4 Afterwards Fiachra came to them, and they asked him the same question, that is to apportion the household of Tara for them, and he said to them he should not judge that until they called to them there one who was wiser and older than him.

"Where is he?" they said.
"Not difficult," he said, "That is Cenfaelad son of Ailill son of Muiredach son of Eogan son of Niall, it is from his head," he said, "that the brain of forgetfulness was removed at the battle of Mag Rath[15] that is with remembrance by him of every thing he

---

[15] Mag rath = possibly field of forts although rath has several meanings

heard of the history of Ireland from then until today. It is correct that he should have a solution for you," he said.

5. Docuas iarum úadib-seom ar cend Chindfháelad ocus dodeachaid side chucu ocus adbertatar a cétna ris béos. Ocus adubairtt Cendfáelad friu, 'Ni dú dúibsi,' arse, 'anní sin do rád frimsa heret bete ar cóic sinser huile for hÉrind.'
'Ca hairm dano itát side?' for fir hÉrind.
'Ní ansa ém,' olse. 'Finchad a Fálmaig Láigen ocus Cú alad a Crúachain Conalad ocus Bran Bairne a Bairind, Dubán mac Dega a cúiced fer Olnegmacht, Túan mac Cairill ó Ultaib, is éside dochuaid isna hilrechtaib.'

5 Afterwards Cenfaelad was sent for and he came to them and they asked the same tale[16] of him. And Cenfaelad answered them, "Not proper for you," he said, "to say to me as long as there are the five other seniors in Ireland."

---

[16] Cetna ris, literally the same story or news. This may read awkwardly to an English audience because 'question' would seem more intuitive here but I am trying to stay true to the original text

"Where then are they?" Said the men of Ireland.

"Not difficult," he said. "Finchad from Falmaig[17], Laigan[18], and Cú Alad[19] from Cruachain[20] Conalad, and Bran Bairne[21] from Bairind[22], Dubán son of Dega[23] from the province of the men of Ol nEgmacht[24], Túan son of Cairill of Ulster, he passed through many shapes."

---

[17] Interestingly falmaig is a form of folmaigid and means to despoil or lay waste to

[18] Leinster

[19] Cú alad, literally 'piebald hound'

[20] Cruachain that is Rath Croghan in Connacht. It is here given as being from Conalad a variant form of the man's name Cu Alad.

[21] Bran means raven, bairne is uncertain but probably means fragments

[22] A form of Bairenn 'rocky district', I would suggest that this is a play on words with bairne, giving us perhaps 'Rocky Raven from Rocky District

[23] Dubán is one of those words with several meanings. Most likely here would be fish-hook I think although given that his father's name Dega probably means 'conflagration or fire' I'd suggest that dubán here may be 'aroused, stirred up', hence 'Arousal son of Conflagration'

[24] Ol = beyond Egmacht= a form of ecmacht meaning powerless

6. Docuas úadib didu for ceand in chóicir sin, ocus tucaid chucu co Temair, ocus doráidset riu a cétna .i. co rocomroinddis dóib tellach Temrach. Roráid iarum cech fer don chóicer sin a chuimne, ocus ba hed roráidset, ní bo dú dóib Temair cona tellach do chomroind heret nobeith a sindser ocus a n-aiti diblínaib in nHérind re dáil an-echtair.

'Cá hairm itá side dino?' ar fir hÉrind.

'Ní ansa,' arsiad: 'Fintan mac Bóchrai meic Betha meic Náei.'

Bái ac Dún Tulcha i Cíarraigi Luachrai.

6 These five were sent for then, and came to them at Tara, and were asked the same, that is how they should partition the household of Tara. Then each man of the five related his memories, and they said, it wasn't proper for them to portion Tara or it's household without their senior and teacher[25] also present in the assembly.

"Where is he then?" said the men of Ireland.

"Not difficult," they said. "Fintan son of Bochra son of Betha son of Noah."

---

[25] Aiti can be read as either foster-father or teacher

He was at Dun Tulcha[26] in Kerry of the rushes

7. Dochoid iarum Berrán gilla Chindfháelad húaidib ar cend Fhindtain co Dún Tulchai re Luachair Deadaid aníar. Ocus roráid a teachtairecht ris. Dodeachaid lais iarum Findtan do Themraig. Ocus isé lín tánic, ocht mbuidne déc .i. nói mbuidne reme ocus nói mbuidne ina díaig, ocus ní roibi andsin acht síl Findtain uile .i. meic ocus húi ocus íarmái ocus indái dó in lucht sin.

7 Afterwards Berrán servant of Cenfaelad went to the chief Fintan at Dun Tulcha west of Luachair Deadaid. And he told him his message. Fintan came with him afterwards to Tara. And a multitude went with him, eighteen companies, that is nine companies behind and nine companies before him and not a one that wasn't of the seed of Fintan, that is his sons and grandsons and great-grandsons and great-great grandsons were in that group.

8. Roferad fáilti mór re Findtan i tig midchuarta, ocus robo fáilid re cách a

---

*ríachtain do cloistin a bríathar ocus a
senchasa. ocus atrachtatar remi huile, ocus
roráidset ris suidi hi cathair bretheman,
ocus adrubairt Findtan friu nocho ragad inti
co fesad a chest. Ocus roráid dino friu,
'nocho riccid a lles lúathgair do chor
immum-sa, ar is tairise lim chena for fáilte
amal is tairise do cach mac a bume, ocus isí
iarum,' ar Fintan, 'mo buime-sea, in indsi-
sea itáthai-si .i. hÉri, ocus is hí a glún
gnáthach na hindsi-sea, in tulach-sa itáthai-
si .i. Temair. Isé didu a mes ocus
murthorud, a bláth ocus a beathamnus inna
hindsi-sea, isé foramroerlongair ó dílind
cusandiu. Ocus am éolach ina fesaib ocus
ina táintib ocus ina toglaib ocus ina
tochmorcaib do neoch dorónad díb ó dílind
ille.'*

Ocus conid andsin doroindi in láid:

8 A great welcome was made for Fintan
in the banqueting house[27] and glad were
they all at his coming and to hear his words
and stories. And they all rose before him and
urged him to sit in the seat of the judge[28] and

---

[27] Midchuarta, literally a banqueting hall of which
the one at Tara was particularly famous

[28] Bretheman, a form of breithem, a person who
judges

Fintan said he would not go until they asked their question. And he said to them, "Not right is so much rejoicing[29] in your hearts for me, for I am as certain of your welcome as every son is of his foster-mother, and this then," said Fintan, "[is] my foster-mother, the island where you are, that is Ireland, and the customary knee of the island is the hill where you are, that is Tara. Moreover her crop[30] and her produce, her flowers and her provisions[31] in this island have supported me from the Deluge[32] until today. And I am learned in her feasts and in her cattle raids, and in her raiding and in her wooing, in everything that has been since the Deluge until now[33].

And then he made this poem:

---

[29] More literally Iles luathgair might be read as 'a multitude of rejoicing' but that's a bit awkward in English in this sentence.

[30] Mes, literally nut crop

[31] Beathamnus can mean everything from food, supplies, produce or cattle

[32] Dilind, the flood of the Bible but may also reference any flood, torrential rain, or the ocean. In this context clearly the first meaning is the one implied.

[33] Ille, literally 'from here' but that is awkward in English.

9. Héiriu cía fhíarfaidir dím
atá lim co grind
cech gabáil rusgob
ó thús bethad bind.

Ireland how [its] enquired of me
It is with me[34] the exactness
Of every taking that has seized her
Since the beginning of the pleasant world

Dia luid anoir Cesair
ingen Beatha in ben
cona cóecait ingen
ocus óen triar fear.

Coming from the east, Cessair
Daughter of Bith, the woman
With her fifty girls[35]
And her single trio of men

Conustarraid díliu
gérbo thrúag in mairg
corus robáid uili
cach duine 'na aird.

They were caught by the Deluge

---

[34] Less literally 'I know'
[35] Literally ingen which can mean daughter or
otherwise girl or maiden

Though it was a miserable sorrow
A measured death for all
Every person on his height[36]

Bith túaith i Sléb Betha
robo trúag in drúim
Ladra i n-Ard Ladrand
Cesair ina cúil.

Bith north in Mount Betha
Miserable was the summit
Ladra in Ard Ladrand
Cessair in her corner

Mad misi romanacht
mac Dé dín úas druinhg
corscib dím in díliu
húas Tul Tuindi truim.

I myself was saved
The son of God's protection over a
throng[37]
The Deluge moved away from me
Over great Tul Tuindi[38]

---

[36] Aird — a high place, elevated
[37] Druinhg a form of drong, a huge crowd or mass
of people
[38] Tul Tuindi — swelling of waves

Blíadain dam fo dílind
re Tul Tuindi tend
nír collad, ní coiteltar
énchollad rob ferr.

A year I was under the Deluge
A time of powerful Tul Tuindi[39]
None have slept, nor will sleep
Better than that sleep

Co namtánic Parrthalón
anoir a tír Gréc
co 'matormailt dam ria síl
cíarbo suthain sét.

Then came Parthalon to me
From the east the land of Greece
Together I was with his progeny
Though it was a long path

Misi i nÉrind fós
sisi hÉri fás
co toracht mac Agnomán
Nemed níamda a nás.

I was myself in Ireland further

---

[39] Given as a place name but can be read as 'a time of powerful swelling waves'; likely a play on words

When Ireland was uninhabited
Until the son of Agamemnon came
Nemed, illustrious his death

Arsin tángadar Fir Bolc
isé in scél find fír
imotormalt damsa friu
cén bátar is tír.

Then came the Fir Bolg
This is a fair, true story
I was together[40] with them
Near them while they were in the land

Fir Bolg is Fir Galión
tancatar ba cían,
tancatar Fir Domnand,
gabsat i nIrruis tiar.

Fir Bolg and Fir Galion
Came, it was a long time after
The Fir Domnann came
They took possession of Irrus in the west

Arsin tángadar Túath Dé
i coepaib cíach cíar
co 'matormuilt damsa friu

---

[40] Imotomalt, imo – together, tormalt a form of
do-meil - consuming

cíar[bo] sáegul cían.

Then came the Tuatha Dé
In dark, misty clouds
Together with them I lived
Though it was a long lifetime[41]

Tángadar meic Míled
iarsin forro i tír
misi i fail cech díne
cosan úair at-chídh.

The sons of Mil came
Afterwards against them in the land
Myself was there beside every generation
Until the hour you see

Iarsain tancatar meic Miled
a hEspain anes
co 'motormalt damsa friu
cíar[bo] thrén a thress.

Afterwards came the sons of Mil
From Spain in the south
Together with them I lived
Though strong was their contention

---

[41] Sáegul – a period of time, a human lifetime, a long amount of time

Doroacht sægul sír
damsa, nocho chel,
co nomtharraid creitem óg
o rig nime nél.

I have reached a long lifetime
For me, without concealment
When the perfected faith came to me
Of the king of cloudy heaven

Is mé Findtan find
mac Bóchra, ní chél,
d'éis na díleand sund
am sruith úasal hér.
Hériu.

I am fair Fintan
Son of Bochra, without concealing,
After the Deluge here
Truly a great, noble[42] elder[43]
Of Ireland

10. 'Is maith sin, a Fhintain,' arsiad. 'Is
ferrde dún cech follugad doberum fort, ocus
is maith lind a fhis úait caidi tairisiu do
chuimne fén.'

---

42 Uasal and ér both can mean noble but each
also has different nuances as well
43   Sruit can be read as elder, sage, ancestor

    'Ní ansa ém,' olse. 'Lod-sa láa tría fid a nÍar-Mumain tíar. Dobiur lim cóer ndeirg do ibur co nusroclandus i llubgort mo lis ocus ásais and co mbad comard fria fer. Nosberim-sa asin lubgurt iarum ocus nosclandaigim forsin faithchi mo lis ceanai, ocus fásais for lár na faithchi sin co namtallad-sa cét láech fo dibli, ocus co namdítned ar gáith ocus ar fhlechad ocus fúacht ocus tes. Roairis ocus roairis mo ibar co 'matormolt dúind, co rolá a duillebar de ar chríne. Antan iarum tallus mo chéill dia thorbu dam chena, dochuas limsa chuici co roleoad dia bun, ocus co ndernait limsa de secht ndabcha ocus secht n-éna ocus secht ndrolmacha ocus secht muidi ocus secht cilairn ocus secht milain ocus secht metair cona cerclaib uile diblínaib. Roairisius-[s]a didu béos ocus mo ibair-lestair ocom co torchradar a circla díb ar críne ocus aesmaire, ocus co roaitherechtha uili limsa co ná ticed acht ían asin dabaig ocus drolmach asan ían ocus muidi asin drolmaig ocus cilarn asin muide ocus milan asin chilarn ocus metar asin milan. Ocus dofunhg-sa do Día uilichumachtach nacon fhetar-sa ca hairm i fail an inadach sin iarna scíth lim ar críne.'

10 "It is good, oh Fintan," they said, "Every man is better for an omission given under you, and it is good for us to know how confident your memory is."

"No difficult thing," he said, "One day I passed through a wood in in the west of Munster from the west[44]. I found by me a red berry of the yew and planted it in the herb-garden of my courtyard and it grew there until it was as high as a man. I took it from the herb-garden afterwards and planted it in the lawn[45] in front my courtyard, and it grew on the middle of the lawn there with room for a hundred warriors under its spreading[46] and with shelter on me from the wind and the rain[47] and cold and heat. I remained and my yew remained nobly together, until its foliage[48] was decayed. I

------

[44] This sounds redundant in English but the original does double emphasize 'west' so I wanted to keep it

[45] Faithchi, a form of faithche meaning a lawn, green, or open expanse in front of a home or city

[46] Dibli is a form of dible which means frenzy. Its connected to duible which means speed. In this context I am choosing to give it as spreading; other translators give it as foliage but I can't see the precedent for that

[47] Flechad, literally 'wetting' a term for rainy weather

went afterwards without hope of turning it to my benefit, I went towards it and cut it off from its base[49] and made from it seven tubs[50] and seven drinking vessels and seven wooden vessels[51] and seven containers[52] and seven pitchers and seven vessels[53] and seven measuring-cups with hoops on all of them. I remained further with my yew vessels until their hoops fell off through decay and old age[54] and I reformed all of them but could get only a drinking vessel from a tub, and a wooden vessel from a drinking vessel, and a container from a wooden vessel, and a pitcher from a container, and a vessel from a pitcher, and a measuring-cup from a vessel.

---

[48] Duillebar = foliage

[49] Bun – literally base of the trunk, source, thick end

[50] Dubcha a form of dabach a large vat or tub with two handles, used for alcohol, water, or washing

[51] Drolmach a type of wooden vessel with rings or handles attached at the side

[52] Muidi, plural of muide, a type of vessel for liquids like milk

[53] Milain, again a specific term for a type of drinking vessel

[54] Crine and aimsaire both can mean old age, with crine additionally having implications of decay. This is another example of the intentional redundance we see throughout this work

And I swear by all-powerful god that I do not know where those replacements were exhausted with me from old age."

11. *'At arrsaig sin samlaid,' ol Diarmaid. 'Is tíachtain tar breith senórach tíachtain tar do breith. Ocus is aire siu didu rotgairmed chucaindi co mad tú noberad breith fír iarum dúind.'*

'Is fír ém,' olse, 'am éolach in cech breithemnos fírén dorónad ó thosuch domuin cosinndiu.' Conid andsin doroindi in láid seo:

11 "Indeed you are venerable," said Dairmuid, "It is opposing[55] the judgment of an elder to oppose your judgement. And it is for that reason we have called you here to us that you should give true judgement to the people here."

"It is true," he said, "I am knowledgeable in every true judgment from the world's beginning until today."

Then he made this poem:

12. *As éol dam sund amne*

---

[55] Tiachtain can also be read as transgression or withdrawal from in this context

ní fuiris nach meraide
cétna breithem, bág cen clith,
ruc cen chinaid in cétbrith.

Knowledge is on me here thus
Without illumination[56] to each fool[57]
The first judge, declaration without hiding,
Spoke without liability the first-judgement

Breth ar díabul úas Druim Den
is éol dam tucht roduced:
rusuc Día dil, delm roleth,
sech fa cétchin ba cétbreth.

Judgement on the Devil over Druim[58] Den
Knowledge is on me of the manner it was given:
Beloved God gave it, tidings spread,
Moreover it was the first crime (and) the first judgement

---

[56] Fuiris is an obscure term but possible a form of for-osna, to illuminate

[57] Meraide – one who is scattered brained or muddle headed according to the eDIL

[58] Druim – height or pinnacle. Den may be a form of denn, colour, but that's speculation.

Tidnocol deoda Dé dil
ara mbeith breth ag dáinib
doridnacht recht bérlai báin
do Moyse mó cech degdáil.

Divine gift of beloved God
So that judgement would be had by
people
Bestowing law of fair language
To Moses greater than every exceptional
law

Dálais Moyse, monar nhglé,
bretha lánmaithi litre
dális Duid iar sene
bretha fíra fáitsine.

Moses bestowed, shining deed,
Fully-good judgment of the letters
David delivered afterwards there
Fair judgments of prophecy

Fénius Farrsaich, faib di rath,
ocus in Cai Cáin-brethach
dorignacht leo, líth nad lacc,
na dá bérlai sechtmogat.

Fenius the Constant, (?)[59] of fortune,

And Cai Cainbrethach[60]
Bestowed by them, festival without weakness,
The seventy two languages

Aimirgen indse Gáedel
ar n-ór, ar n-án, ar n-óebel
Aimirgen Glúngel co ngoil
ruc in chétbreith im Themair.

Amergin of the island of the Gael
Our gold, our splendour, our spark,
Amergin White-knee with valour
Made the first-judgement on Tara

Trí ríg i lLiathdruim na ler
ocus cethri meic Mílead
sínset im tuinithi thend
indse airegda hÉrend.

Three kings in Liathdruim[61] of the sea
And the four sons of Míl
They forwarded strong possession
Of the pre-eminent island of Ireland

---

[59] Faib is a word of uncertain meaning

[60] Cai = way or path, Cain-brethach = judgement-of-Law

[61] Liathdruim – liath = grey, druim = hill or ridge, hence 'grey ridge'

As and ruc Aimirgin dóib
in breith fírecnaid fírchóir
meic Míled do dul amach
dar nói tonna ar muir medrach.

It was there Aimergin spoke to them
The right and genuine judgment
The sons of Míl should go outwards
Between the ninth wave on the joyous[62]
sea

Brogsad iarsin for sáile
cethri meic ríg Espáine
co radnacht leo, líth úas tuind
Dond co fárcbaid ós Tig Duind.

They put out to sea[63]
Four sons of the king of Spain
Buried by them, a festival over the
waves,
    Donn, left at Tech Duinn[64]

Co fárcbad iar gail gúir glicc

---

[62] Medrach – according to the eDIL a common
adjective applied to the sea or ocean, meaning
mirthful, joyous, merry
[63] Sáile, the sea, literally seawater or brine
[64] Tech Duinn, the house of Donn

hÍr in n-úir scenbluind Scellicc.

They left after furious, valiant warlike ardour
Ir in the rough sharp soil of the crag

Scuichsit iarsin soir na slóigh
Émer ocus Éremóin
corgobsad iar ndíth a ne[i]rt
hÉrind iar n-élod Egeipt.

Afterwards, escaped eastwards the hosts
Of Emer and Eremon
Suffering the destruction of their forces
Ireland after escaping Egypt

Arsin rogénair in gein
hÍsu ó Muiri ingein
co tárfad breatha co mbail
tria núfiadhnaise nóemgloin.

Thereafter the birth was produced
Jesus from the maiden Mary
And judgements were declared with goodness
Through the pure New Testament

As leór so do solbraib sreth
barr beg do gnímaib cáinbreth
co fheastais buidne brasa

comsid éolach éolusa.

This is sufficient alliteration of eloquence
Small crown of the deed of good
judgments
That henceforth boastful hosts should
Be capable of learning knowledge

13. *'Maith sin, a Fhindtain,' arsiad, 'is ferrdi dún do thíachtain do thurim sheanchasa hÉrend.'*

'Am mebrach-sa ém,' ollse, 'I sreathaib senchusa hÉrend indus robas indte cosin n-uair-se, ocus indus bether indti béos co bráth.'

'Ceist,' arsiad, 'can as rothucais-seo sin, ocus cid as neasom diar cobair-ne den tshencha[s] sin immoní imráidim im suidigud tellaich Themrach?'

'Ni ansa,' ar Fintan. 'Indisfet-sa dúibse colléc ní deside'

13 "Good then, oh Fintan," they said, "It is better we are with your arrival to tell the story of Ireland."

"I remember indeed," he said, "the order of the ancient history of Ireland, how it has been until this hour and how it will be until Judgement."

"A question," they said, "where have you acquired that and what is needful to assist us of this history to consider in settling the household of Tara?"

"Not hard," said Fintan. "I will tell to you however something else."

14. ' ' *Bámar-ni feachtus i mmórdáil fer nÉreand sund im Chonaing Begeclach im ríg nErend. Láa n-and dúin isin dáil sin iarum co n-acamar in scálfher mór cáin cumachtach chucaind aníar la fuinead nhgréne. Donbert ingantas mór méd a delba. Comard fri fid máel a dá gúaland, ecnach nem ocus grían fo gabal ara fhot ocus ara cháime. Fíal étrocht glainidi imme amal étach línda lígda. Dá máelasa imma chosaib ocus ní feas cía luib dia rabadar. Monhg legta órbuidi fochas fair co clár a dá leas. Taibli lecda inna láim cli, cróeb co trí toirthib ina láim deis, itté trí toraid robádar fuirre, cnóe ocus ubla ocus dercain i cétemun sin. ocus ba hanabaid cech torad díb. Dochechaing sechond iarum morthimchell na hairechtai ocus a c[h]róeb órda illdathach do fhid Lebáin ria ais, co n-ebairt fer úaindi fris, 'Tadall lat,' arse, 'co roaicilli in ríg .i. Conaing mBececlach.'*

Frisrogart-som co n-érbairt, 'Cid is ailicc dúib húam,' arse.

'Co fesamar úait,' arsiat, 'can dodeachaid ocus cid thége ocus caidi th'ainm ocus caidi do slondud.'

14 "There was an occasion of a great-assembly of the men of Ireland around Conaing[65] Beg-Eclach[66] the king of Ireland. That day in the assembly there we saw approaching a great giant[67], fair and powerful, coming from the west at the setting of the sun. We were inspired with wonder at the great size of his form. Equally high as a wood the roundness of his two shoulders, the sky and sun visible under his thighs[68] for his length and beauty. A shining crystal veil[69] like a covering around him of

---

[65] A form of Aingid, meaning to protect

[66] Begeclach, literally 'little fear'

[67] Scálfher is usually given as giant but may also be read as 'great hero'. Scál is usually a phantom or supernatural being but may also be applied to humans or heroes. Interestingly written in reverse order as Ferscál the understood meaning would be 'human man'

[68] Gabal is a tricky word that literally means fork or forking but is used idiomatically for several things including thighs

[69] Interesting to note that a very similar description is used for Moses, perhaps meant here to imply the holiness or wisdom of the character being introduced

bright linen. Two sandals on his feet and its unknown what they were of. Flowing hair of yellow-gold in waves to the level of his thighs. Tablets of stone in his left hand, a branch wit three fruits on his right hand, these were the three fruits on it, nuts and apples and acorns in Mayday[70] on it. And unripe was every fruit on it. He strode past us going around the assembly and his many-colored golden branch of Lebanon wood[71] behind him, and one man said to him, "Visit with us," he said, "speak with the king that is Conaing Bececlach."

He answered and said, "What speech would you have with me?" he said.

"Whence have you come [from] and where are you going and what is your name and what is your surname?"

15. *'Dodechaid-sa ém,' arse, 'ó fuined ocus tégim do thurgbáill, ocus isé m'ainm Tréfhuilngid Tre-eochair.'*
'Cid diatá duit-seo int ainm hí sein,' arsiat.

---

[70] Cétemun a form of Céitemain, May first, May day

[71] Possibly cedar?

*'Ní ansa,' arse. 'Dáig is mé immofoilnge
turcbáil nhgréine ocus a fuiniud.'*

*'Ocus cid dodtuc dond fuiniud mas oc
turcbáil bí?'*

*'Ní ansa,' arse. 'Fer imrinodair .i.
rocrochad le hIúdaidib indiu, rochechaing
iarum tairsiu taréis in gníma, ocus ní
rothaitne friu, et ised domfucsa co fuiniud
dia fhis cid robái grían, conid andsin dam,
ocus ó rofhetar cindus tíri dar-si fuiniud co
rochtus iarum inis nGlúairi iar nIrrus
Domnand ocus ní fúair tír ó sein síar, ar
isedh sin tairrsech darsa fuineann grían
amail isé tarsech darsa turcbháill pardhus
Ádhaim.'*

15 "I have come, indeed," he said, "from
sunset and I go to sunrise and my name is
Tréfhuilngid[72] Tre-eochair[73]."

"How has it come to be on you the name
for yourself?" they said.

"Not difficult," he said, "Because of me
is caused the rising of the sun and its
setting."

"And how have you come to the setting if
the rising is where you should be?"

---

[72] Tréfuilngid – uncertain but probably related to
upholding or supporting

[73] Treochair – three cornered, a type of metre

"Not difficult," he said, "A man who was tortured, that is crucified with the Jews today, it then stepped past them after that action and it wasn't visible to them, this is what brought me to the setting to know what [caused] the sun to be so, and then it was revealed to me and I knew in what land it sets so I came afterwards to the island of Glauri beyond Irrus Domnann and no cold land beyond itself westwards because there is the boundary where the sun sets just as the boundary of its rising is the paradise of Adam."

16. *'Abraid-si iarum,' arse, 'can bar cenél ocus cuin dodechaidbar isin indsi-se.'*
'Ní ansa,' ar Conaing Bececlach. 'De cloind Míled Espáine dúindi, ocus do Grécaib ar mbunad; iar cumtach Thúir Nemrúaid, ocus iar cumasc na n-ilbérlae dochuamar i nEigeipt fo chuiriud Foraind ríg Eigipte. Nél mac Féniusa ocus Góedel Glas roptar hé ar tóisich airet bámar theas. Conid de dogarar díndi Féne ó Fénius .i. Féne, ocus Gáeidel 'ga rádh ó Gáedel Glas amail adbertar:'
   Féni ó Fénius adberta,
   bríg cen dochta
   Gáeidil ó Gáedel Glas garta
   Scuit ó Scota.

*'Scota didu ingen Foraind ind ríg
dobreth side do mhnái do Niul mac Féniusa
ar ndul i nEigept. Conid hí ar senmáthair-ne
ocus conid húaidi didu dogairter díndi
Scuit.'*

16 "Speak then," he said, "What is your
nation and whence have you come to this
island?"

"Not difficult," said Conaing Bececlach.
"From the children of Miles of Spain's
people and from Greece is our origin; after
the constructing of the Tower of Nimrod and
after the mixing of many languages we came
into Egypt under invitation of Pharaoh King
of Egypt. Nél son of Féniusa and Green
Goedel where our chiefs while we were in
the south. So we are called Fene from
Fenius that is the Fene and Gael from Green
Gaedel as was said:

The Feni from Fenius are called,
Strength without withholding
The Gael from generous Green Gaedel
The Scots from Scota

Scota, daughter of Pharaoh the king, was
given as wife to Nel son of Fenius on going
into Egypt. So that she is our grandmother
and so that from her we are called Scots."

17. *'Isind aidchi iarum, arse, i nn-érlatar meic hIsrael asind Egept, dia ndechadar cosaib tirmaib tria Muir Rúaidh la prímthóisech túaithi Dé .i. la Moyse mac Ambra, ocus dia robáidhedh Forand cona shlúag issin muir sin ic fastadh [na] nAbraidi ina ndóiri, húair dodechaid ar senathair-ne iarum la hEigeptacdai for íarraid túaithi Dé, atraigsetar ferg Fhoraind friu dia torsed for cúlu, is cid intan ná torsed Forand chucu atraigsetar in Eigeptacdai dia ndóerad amail rodóersat meic hIsrael fecht n-aili. Co roélaisead isind ai[d]chi fa deich lonhgaib do libernaib Foraind for muincind Mara Rúaid aran aicen nemforcennach ocus timchell domhain fo thúaith síar sech slébe Cucais sech Scithia sech India dar mu[i]r and .i. Muir Chaisp, darna Gáethlaigib Meotacdai sech Eoraip anairr-deas síar-des iar Muir Torrén, lám chlé re hAfraic sech Columna Hercail co hEspáin, a hEspáin iartanaib isan indsi-se.'*

17 "Afterwards in the night then," he said, "when the children of Isreal escaped from Egypt, when they went with dry feet through the Red Sea with the premier leader[74]

---

[74] Prímthóisech – prim – first, primary Tóisech –

of People of God[75], that is with Moses son of Abraham, and when Pharoah and his host were drowned in the sea there having detained the Hebrews in slavery, because our ancestors[76] had not gone with the Egyptians in pursuit of the People of God, they dreaded Pharoah's wrath against them should he return, and even if Pharoah should not return they dreaded that the Egyptians should enslave them as they had the sons of Israel on other occasions. And so they escaped in the night on ten ships [that were] galleys of Pharoah through the strait[77] of the Red Sea upon the boundless[78]s ocean and around the world north west beyond India the ocean on the ocean there that is the

---

first, main, leading

[75] Túaithi Dé – given here as people of god but widely used in other texts for the Tuatha De Danann. Its been speculated that the 'Danann' was a later add on to Tuath De Danann to distinguish them from the biblical term we see here, which was likely a later addition that created conflict with the older term.

[76] Senathair literally grandfathers but in this context meaning ancestors or forefathers

[77] Muincind, literally 'neck-head' indicating an inlet or straight or narrow strip of land

[78] Nemforcennach nem – without forcennach ending, hence limitless, boundless

Caspian Sea, secondly the Meaotic Marshes beyond Europe south east to south west along the sea of Torren[79], left hand to Africa beyond the Columns of Hercules to Spain, from Spain further to this island here."

18. 'Ocus ind Espáin,' ar Tréfuilingid, 'cade a tír sund?'

'Ní ansa, ed ardradairc,' ar Conaing, 'úan fa deas atá, air is a radurc atconnairc Ith mac Breoguin Slébe Irruis deiscirt de mullach Thuir Breogain a hEasbáin ocus isé thánic do thaiscélad forsin n-indsi-sea re maccaib Mílead, ocus is fora slicht dodeachamair-ne inte isind nómad blíadna iar tíachtain na nIsraeldae dar Muir Rúaid.'

18 "And in Spain," said Trefuilingid, "where is this land?"

"Not difficult, the great prospect," said Conaing. "is from us to the south, it is by viewing that Ith son of Breogun saw the mountains of the land of Irruis from the height of the tower of Breogun in Spain and it is he who came and spied on the island here for the sons of Mil and on his track we came to this island nine years after the

---

[79] Mediterranean

escape[80] of the Israelites through the Red Sea."

19. *'Cía bar lín-se is[in] indsi-se?' ar Tréfhuilngid: 'robad maith limsa for n-aiscin ind-óenbaile.'*

'Ní fil ém diar n-úaiti,' ar Conaing, 'ocus mad áil duitsiu atetha sin, acht is dóig lim bid sním leisna dáini do fhulanhg-su frisin ré sin.'

'Nocho ba sním,' arse, 'ar romfiurfusa bolad ina cróibi-sea fil am'láimh do bhiudh ocus do dhigh heret bam béo.'

19 "How many number you in this island?" said Trefuilngid, "It would be good to me to see you in one place."

"We are not few," said Conaing, "And if you wish it[81] you will obtain it there. But it is likely to me to cause anxiety with the people to be supporting you through that time there."

"Have no anxiety," he said, "because the chief-miraculous[82] scent of the branch in my

---

[80] Tíachtain may also be read as coming, reaching, or passing

[81] Literally 'if a wish is on you'

[82] Rom — chief or primary fiurt — wonder or miracle

hand gives to me food and my drink for the length of my life."

20. *Anais iarum octhaib xl. láa ocus aidchi co rotinólta fir hÉrenn dó frisin ré sin co Temhraigh, ocus confhaca uili ind-óenbhaili conid iarum roróidh-sem riu, 'Cad iat libse,' arse, 'ailgi comgni fer nÉreand i rrígthich Themra, taisfenaid dún.'*
'Ní rabadar ém,' arsiad, 'seanchaidi farrsaidi occainne frisin lámmais ailgi choimgni co tánoc-sa chucund.'
'Robarbia-si ón húaimse,' arse, 'rodosuidighiub-sa dúib sreith seanchusa ocus ailgi chomgni tellaich Temrach fésin co ceithri hardaib hErenn imbi, ar is mesea in fíada fíréolach foillsiges cech n-ainfis do chách.'

20 He remained thereafter with them for forty days and nights while the men of Ireland gathered there during that time at Tara and he saw them all in one place so afterward he said to them, "What have with you," he said, "of records of historical knowledge[83] of the men of Ireland in the royal household of Tara, exhibit them to us."

---

[83] Coimgne, a branch of learning specific to historical records or knowledge

"We have none," they said, "wise storytellers to whom we could trust the records of historical knowledge until you had come to us."

"You shall have that from me," he said, "I will establish for you the order of stories and historical records of the settlement of Tara itself with the four heights of Ireland surrounding, because I am the truly-wise witness[84] who manifests all knowledge to everyone."

21. *'Tucaid iarum chucam-sa mórfesear cecha hairdi i nÉirind do neoch is mó ergna díb ocus is mó gáes ocus glicus béos ocus seanchaidi ind ríg fadesin fileat for tellach Temrach, ar is ceathar-aird as chóir chum fhodail na Temrach ocus a comgni, co ruca cech mórfeisiur díb a chuit chóir dona hailgib comgni sin thellaich Themra.'*

21 "Bring then to me the wisest from every quarter of Ireland, who are each the most discriminating, and who are the most intelligent and cleverest yet and the storytellers[85] of the king himself from the

---

[84] Fíada may be read as knower, witness, or person who gives testimony

[85] Seanchaidi, anglicized shanachie

household of Tara, for the four-quarters are right to be at the dividing of Tara and its histories, that each wise-one should take their correct share of the histories there of the household of Tara.

22. Roaicellastar iarum for leith na seanchaidi sin co n-érbairt friu ailgi comgne cecha harda dond hÉrind. Acus is iarsin iarum adbert-som risin ríg .i. re Conaing, 'Tairr-siu,' arse, 'fén I fechtus-sa for leith, co n-éiciu[s]-sa duit ocus do formna fer nÉrind immut co fodailseam-ni hÉrind indus rosndlumus dona ceithri móirfeisir feassaraib chucut.'

Roindis iarum doridisi dóib uili i coitciund, ocus is rimsa, ar Fintan, rohérbad ar eisnéis ocus a acallaim fiad int shlúag, ar is misi seanchaidh bad siniu fúair ara chind i nHérind. Ar bá-sa i Tul Tuindi fri ré inna dílenn, ocus robo m'óenur inti iar nhdílind co ceann dá blíadna ar míle eret robúi Ériu fás. ocus robá-sa iarsin i comaimsir re cech ndíne rusgab ó sin cosin lá-sa i tánic Tréfhuilngid dond oirecht-sa Conaing Bececlaig conid ó sin rofhiarfaid Tréfuilngid dímsa tria fhis imchomairc:

22 He addressed afterwards the storytellers to the side[86] there and told them every history of the quarters of Ireland. And afterwards he said to the king, that is Conaing, "Come you," he said, "yourself for a time to the side, so I may make it known to you and to the wide men of Ireland how Ireland was partitioned as I have related it to the four groups of wise-ones there."

He related it all again to these others equally[87] and it was to me, said Fintan, entrusted to be related and for telling in the presence of the host, because I was the oldest storyteller to be found before him in Ireland. Because I was in Tul Tuinde in the time before the Deluge, and I was alone there after the Deluge for two and a thousand years when Ireland was uninhabited[88]. And I have been afterwards contemporary with every people who have taken [Ireland] there until the day that Tréfuilngid came to the assembly of Conaing Bececlaig so that Tréfuilngid questioned me through his knowledge of enquiry:

---

[86] Leith a form of leth, side but can also be read as apart of individually

[87] Coitciund – in generally, equally

[88] Fás – uninhabited, deserted, empty

23. *'A Findtain,' arse, 'ocus Éri cía gabad ca rabad inde?'*

'Ní ansa,' ar Fintan, 'Íaruss fis. tuadus cath. airthis bláth. teissus séis. fortius flaith.'

'Is fír ém, a Findtain,' ar Tréfhuilngid, '' at senchaid saineamail. Is amlaid robái ocus bias co bráth béos, .i.

23. 'Oh Fintan,' said he, 'and Ireland, how has it been divided, how is it therein?'

'Not difficult,' said Fintan, 'In the west knowledge. In the north battle, in the east renown.

In the south melody. Above her sovereignty.'

'This is true, oh Fintan,' said Tréfuilngid, 'You are an excellent historian.

Thus it is and shall be forever, that is

24. *A fis, a forus, a foirceatol, a bág, a breithemnus, a comgne, a cómairle, a scéla, a seanchasa, a sos, a sodelb, a sulbairi, a háine, a himdercadh, a gart, a himed, a hindmus asa híarthur aníar.'*

'Can as aidi?' bar in slúag.

'Ní ansa,' arse. 'A hÁe, a hUmull, a hAidhne, a Bairind, a Briuuss, a Breithfne, a Brí Airg, a Bearramain, a Bagnu, a Cera, a

Corund, a Cruachain, a hIrrus, a hImga, a hImgan, a Tarbgu, a Teidmmu, a Tulchaib, a Muaid, a Muirisc, a Meada, a Maigib .i. etar Traigi ocus Reocha ocus Lacha, a Mucrumu, a Maenmaig, a Maig Luirg, a Maig Ene, a hAraind, a hAigliu, a hAirtiuch.'

24. Her knowledge, her stability, her teaching, her boldness, her judgments, her likeness, her advice, her stories, her histories, her resting, her beautiful form, her eloquence, her brilliance, her insulting, her generosity, her bounty, her ardour from the western part of the west.'

'Whence are these?' said the assembly.

'Not hard' said he. 'from Áe, from Umall, from Aidne, from Bairenn, from Bres, from Breithfne, from Brí Airg, from Bearramain, from Bagna, from Cera, from Corann, from Cruachan, from Irrus, from Imga, from Imgan, from Tarbga, from Teidmne, from Tulcha, from Muad, from Muiresc, from Meada, from Maigib that is between Traigi and Reocha and Lacha, from Mucrama, from Maenmag, from Mag Luirg, from Mag Ene, from Arann, from Aigle, from Airtech.'

25. *'A catha, immorro,'* arse, *'ocus a comrama, a dúiri, a drobela, a drenna, a díumasa, a dímáine, a húaill, a hallud, a hindsaigthi, a crúas, a coicthi, a congala, asa tuaiscert atúaid.'*

'Can a[s] suidiu?' ar in sluag.

'Ní ansa. A lLiu, a lLurg, a lLothur, a Callaind, a Fearnmaig, a Fidhgha, a Sruib Bruin, a Bernus, a Dabull, a hAird Fhothaid, a Gull, a hIrgull, a Airmmuch, a Glennaib, a Geraib, a Gabur, a hEamain, a hAiliuch, a hImchlar.'

25. 'As well her battles,' he said, 'and her contests, her strongholds, her rough roads, her combats, her arrogance, her vanity, her pride, her glory, her aggressiveness, her bravery, her fifths, her valours, from the northern part of the north.'

'Whence are the aforementioned?' said the assembly.

'Not hard. From Lie, from Lorg, from Lothar, from Callain, from Farney, from Fidga, from Sruib Brain, from Bernas, from Daball, from Ard Fothaid, from Goll, from Irgoll, from Airmmach, from the Glens, from Gera, from Gabur, from Emain, from Ailech, from Imclar.'

26. *'A bláth dino,' arse, 'ocus a beathamnass, a ceasa, a cosnuma, a cleas n-airm, a noethaighi, a halle, a hingantai, a sobés, a sochostud, a háinis, a himid, a horddan, a tráchta, a turcharthi, a teglochus, a hilldána, a hinaltus, a hilmáine, a sróll, a síric, a sítai, a bri(t)graighi, a bre[cc]glas, a brugamnos asa hairthear anoir.'*

'Can as suide?' ar in sluag.

'Ní ansa ém,' olse. 'A Fethuch, a Fothnu, a hInrechtro, a Mugno, a Biliu, a Bairniu, a Bernaib, a Drendaib, a Druach, a Diamair, a Leib, a lLiniu, a Laithirni, a Cuib, a Cúailgiu, a Cind Chon, a Maig Roth, a Maig Inis, a Muig Muirthemne.'

26. 'Her flowering as well,' said he, 'and her supplies, her spears, her protection, her weapons-feats, her householders, her praises, her wonders, her morality, her good manners, her splendour, her enclosures, her honour, her strength, her wealth, her householding, her multitude of arts, her attendants, her many treasures, her banners, her fine fabrics, her silks, her riding horses, her young trout, her hospitality, from the eastern part of the east.'

'Whence the aforementioned?' said the assembly.

'Not hard indeed,' said he. 'from Fethach, from Fothna, from Inrechtra, from Mugna, from Bile, from Bairne, from Berna, from Drenna, from Druach, from Diamar, from Lee, from Line, from Lathirne, from Cuib, from Cooley, from Cenn Con, from Mag Rath, from Mag Inis, from Mag Muirthemne.'

27. *'A hesa, a hóenaigi, a donda, a derga, a súithi, a cruithnecht, a céolchairecht, a bindis, a hairfideadh, a hecna, a hairmitniu, a séis, a foglaim, a foirceatul, a fiansa, a fidchelacht, a déne, a díscere, a filidecht, a fechemnus, a féle, a forus, a tascor, a torthaigi asa descert andeas.'*

'Can as suidi?' arsiat.

'Ní ansa,' ar Tréfuilngid. 'A Mairg, a Maistin, a Raighniu, a Rúirind, a Gabair, a Gabran, a Clíu, a Cláiriu, a Femhniudh, a Faifaiu, a Bregon, a Barcaib, a Cind Chailli, a Clériu, a Cermnu, a Raithlind, a Gleannamain, a Gobair, a Lúachair, a Labraind, a Loch Léin, a Loch Lugdach, a Loch Daimdeirg, a Cathair Chonrái, a Cathair Cairbri, a Cathair Ulad, a Dún

*Bindi, a Dún Cháin, a Dún Tulcha, a Fertae,
a Feoraind, a Fiandaind.'*

27. 'Her flowing streams, her fairs, her
nobles, her redness, her knowledge, her
wheat, her music-making, her harmony, her
entertainment, her wisdom, her respect, her
melody, her learning, her instruction, her
warrior-bands, her fidchell playing, her
swiftness, her boldness, her poetry, her
patronage, her science, her stability, her
King's retinue, her fruitfulness from the
southern part of the south.'

'Whence the aforementioned?' they said.

'Not hard,' said Tréfulngid. 'From
Mairg, from Maistiu, from Raigne, from
Rairiu, from Gabair, from Gabran, from
Clíu, from Claire, from Femhne, from
Faifae, from Bregan, from Barchi, from
Cenn Chaille, from Clére, from Cermna,
from Raithlinn, from Glennamain, from
Gobair, from Lúachair, from Labrand, from
Loch Léin, from Loch Lugdach, from Loch
Daimdeirg, from Cathair Chonroi, from
Cathair Cairbri, from Cathair Ulad, from
Dún Bindi, from Dún Cháin, from Dún
Tulcha, from Fertae, from Feorainn, from
Fiandainn.'

28. *'A rrígi, uero, a rechtairi, a hordan, a hoireochuss, a cobsaidi, a conhgbála, a fuilngeda, a forrána, a cathaigi, a cairpthigi, a fiandus, a flaithemnas, a hardrigi, a hollamnas, a mid, a maithiuss, a ciurm, a clothaigi, a rroblad, a rathmaire, asa meadón.'*

'Can as suidi?' arsiat.

'Ní ansa,' ar Tréfuilngid. 'A Midiu, a Biliu, a Bethriu, a Bruidin, a Colbu a Cnodbu, a Cuillind, a hAilbiu, a hAsul, a hUissniuch, a Sídán, a Sleamain, a Sláine, a Cnu, a Cernu, a Cenandus, a Brí Scáil, a Brí Graigi, a Brí meic Thaidg, a Brí Foibri, a Brí Díli, a Brí Fremhaindi, a Temair, a Teathfa, a Teamair Broga Niadh, a Temair Breg, a forbflaithius for Érind uili eistib sin.'

28. 'Her kings, as well, her administrators, her honour, her leading nobles, her stability, her maintaining, her champions, her aggressions, her warriors, her charioteers, her war-bands, her sovereignty, her high Kings, her highest poets[1], her renown, her excellence, her fame, her great glory, her prosperity, from the centre.'

'Whence the aforementioned?' they said.

'Not hard,' said Tréfulngid. 'From Meath, from Bile, from Bethre, from Bruiden, from Colba from Cnodba, from Cuilliu, from Ailbe, from Asal, from Uisneach, from Sídán, from Slemain, from Sláine, from Cno, from Cerna, from Cennandas, from Brí Scáil, from Brí Graigi, from Brí meic Tadg, from Brí Foibri, from Brí Dín, from Brí Fremain, from Tara, from Tethba, from Teamair Broga Niadh, from Temair Breg, the landed sovereignty of all Ireland from these.'

29. *Fácbais iarum Tréfhuilngid Tre-eochair firu hÉrend fon n-ordugud sin co bráth, ocus fácbais ní do chóeraib inna cróibi bái inna láim oc Fintan mac Bóchra conasrola-side isna hinadaib in robo dóig leis a nn-ás i nHérind, ocus ité craind rofásait isna cóeraib sin: Bili Tortan, ocus Eó Rosa, Eó Mugna ocus Cróeb Daithi ocus Bili nUissnig. Ocus airis Fintan ic sloind seanchassa do fheraib hÉrenn co mbo hé ba hiarlathi dona bilib, ocus co racrínsad ria lind. Ó roairig iarum Findtan a sentaith fén ocus sentaith na mbili is and doróne in láid:*

29 Afterwards Trefuilngid Tre-eochair left the men of Ireland under this arrangement[89] there forever, and left some of the berries from the branch in his hand with Fintan mac Bochra so that he could plant them in the places of Ireland where they might grow, and these are the trees which grew from those berries: the great tree[90] of Tortu and the yew[91] of Ross, the yew of Munga and tree of Daithi and great tree of Usnech. And Fintan dallied telling stories with the men of Ireland until he was a survivor beyond these trees and the last of them withered. So that afterwards Fintan perceived his own old age and the old age of the trees there he made this poem:

30. Is fodeirc damsa indiu
maten moch iar n-uréirgiu
a Dún Tulcha tíar doráith
húachtur bar[r] fedha Lebáin.

It is visible to me today
In the early morning after arising

---

[89] That is, the description he has given of the provinces

[90] Bile indicates a large, ancient, or venerated tree

[91] Eo, a yew tree although it may also mean any large tree or shaft. In other translations this is given simply as tree however I am choosing to go with the implicit meaning of a yew.

From Dun Tulcha, west of the fort,
Over the top of the forest of Lebenon

Missi a debrad am fer sean
am leisciu ar cách re tairdead
hisí is cían ó tib dig
dílind ós imlind Usnig.

Myself, by God's doom, I am an old man
I am more reluctant than ever for the
(great-guide)[92]
And it is long since the destruction of the
rejected
The Deluge over the centre of Usneach

Bili Tortan Eó Rosa
at comáille comdosa
Mugna is Cróeb Daithi indiu
is Fintan a n-iarlaithiu.

The great tree of Tortu and the yew of
Ross
Of equal beauty, of equal bushiness[93]

---

[92] Tairdead is glossed in an issue of Eriu as
hairdfhedh which I am interpreting as ard – high or
great and fed -guide. This is entirely suppositional on
my part and tardead is usually left untranslated
[93] Comdosa means 'as bushy as'

[the yew of] Mugna and tree of Daithi
today
  And Fintan is the survivor

Eas Rúaid heret aiges núall
cén beit eicne 'ga imlúad
Dún Tulcha cos toraich mair
ní scéra re deg-seanchaid.

As long as Ess[94] Ruaid[95] loudly flows[96]
While salmon are active there
Dun Tulcha, where the sea reaches
Will never be without a good storyteller

Am seanchaid fén fiadh cech dronhg
deich cét blíadna cen imroll
re ré mac Mílead, mét neirt,
robsam fiadnaiseach fodeirc.

I am a storyteller myself in the presence
of every crowd[97]

---

[94] Ess means a white water area of a river or
rapidly flowing area

[95] Ruaid literally means dark or brownish red but
is used poetically to mean strong or formidable. Ess
Ruaid then may be read roughly as 'Formidable
Rapids'

[96] Aiges here, a form of aigid, more properly
reads as drives or impels but that is difficult to
render in English in this context

Ten hundred years without an error
Before the time of the sons of Míl,
greatness of strength,
And I bear visible witness.

*31. Doróne iarum in láid sin, ocus roairis
re sloind senchasa do fheraib hÉrind béos
conice in inbaid sin tánic fo gairm Diarmata
meic Cerbaill ocus Fland Foebla meic
Scandláin ocus Chindfháelad meic Aililla
ocus fer nÉrenn ar chena do brith breithi
dóib im Suidigud tellaig Themra.*
   *Acus así breth ruc dóib: 'a bith amail
dosairnicmair,' ar Findtan, 'ní thargom tara
n-ordugud forfhácaib Tréfhuilngid Tre-
eochair remum, ar ba haingel Dé héside, nó
fa Día féisin.'*

31 He made then this poem there and he
met[98] to relate stories to the men of Ireland,
further he remained he remained for that
time there until he came at the summons of

---

[97] Drong indicates an uncounted number of
people, a crowd, a grouping

[98] Airis can be read as arranged to meet (its used
in the past tense here) but is also used to mean a
tryst or assignation, as well as in the phrase airis
Catha 'meet in battle', indicating perhaps a more
personal or intimate type of meeting as opposed to a
general meeting

Dairmat son of Cerbal and Fland son of Scandlan and Cindfaelad son of Ailill and the men of Ireland as well to give judgment to them on the arranging of the household of Tara. And this was his judgment on it: "Let it be the same as we have found," said Fintan, "We will not go against the arrangement bestowed by Trefuilngid Tre-eochair before, as he was an angel of god, or perhaps god himself."

32. Tángadar iarsein mathi hÉrenn amail roráidsem do t[h]idnocol Fintain co hUisneach, conid and rochelebair cach díb di arailiu i mmulluch Usnig. Ocus rosuigid ina fiadnaisi lia cloichi cóic-druimneach i fír-mullach Uisnig. Ocus dobert drumain de fri cech cóiced in-nHérind, ar is amlaid atá Temair ocus hUisnech i nHerind amail bit a di áraind a mmíl indile. Ocus co tóraind forrach and .i. irrondus cach cóiced díb in-hUisnech ocus doroindi Fintan in láid so iar córugud ind lia :

32 The nobility of Ireland came afterwards as has been said escorting Fintan to Uisneach, and there they each parted from each other on the top of Uisneach. And he gave in their presence a standing stone to five ridges[99] to the chief-men in Uisneach,

so thus are Teamhair and Uisneach in
Ireland like the two kidneys an animal
possesses. And he marked a measure of land
there that is a territory to every province of
them in Uisneach and Fintan made this
poem after arranging the stones:

33. Cóic hurrunda Érind
iter muir is tír
adfesar a cóicricha
cecha huirruind díb.

Five portions of Ireland
Both sea and land
Their borders will be told
Each portion of them

Ó Drobáis drongadbail
deis Bealach Cúairt
co Boïnd mborrfadaig
sruth Segsa súairc.

From Drobais[100] place-of-herds

---

[99] Cóic-druimneach is given in other translations
as the five provinces but there's no clear precedent
of translating druimneach – literally curved or
ridged, often used for geographical ridges – as
provinces. I am choosing here to give the more
literal meaning rather than an interpretation that
seems to be speculative

South of Bealach Cuairt[101]
Towards the swelling Boyne
Segais's cheerful stream

Ó Boïnd bánsrothaig
co cétaib cúan
co Comar ndál-buidneach
Thri nUsci n-úar.

From the white-streamed Boyne
With a hundred harbours
Towards Comar of the Hosts
Cold Tri-Usci[102]

Ón Chomar chétna-sin
co fuiritiud cas
co Beolo na n-anhgbaid-Chon
dangairther glass.

That same Comar there
With twisted (?)[103]
Towards the Pass of the fierce Hound
Called Glass[104]

---

[100] The Drowes between Donegal and Leitrim, source: eDIL

[101] Bealach = roadway, cuairt = circular, round

[102] Tri-Usci = three-waters

[103] Fuirtiud has an unknown meaning

[104] Glass, properly glas, is a term for any colour from grey to green to light blue. Cú glas, literally

Ón Belach Conglais [sin]
cruthach in gen
co Luimneach lethanglas
frismbarca ben.

From the Pass of the Foreigner there[105]
Beautiful the smile
Towards broad-green Luimneach
Which beats against ships

Ó purt ind Luimnig-sin
luiben glass clár
co Drobáis nduillendglais
fris mbenand sál.

From the port of Luimneach there
Green-fringed plain
Towards green-leafed Drobais[106]
Against the beating sea

Súithemail slechtoghud
frisogar súitt

'grey wolf' is a term for a foreign warrior or foreigner more generally. 'Fierce Hound called Glass' is likely a poetic reference to the cú glas here, hence 'pass of the fierce foreigner'. This is supported by the next line which directly calls it Pass of the Cú Glas.

[105] See previous footnote
[106] See footnote 100

comlán in certugud
dia cor i cóic.
Cóic.
Roinde na n-ardchúiced
ind-Uisnech rúitt
randsait tall tri[i]t
ind licc i cúic.
Cúic.

Agreeable division
Which the roads have achieved
Perfect the arrangement
Being placed into five.
Five.
The points of the great-provinces
To Uisnech go
They divided that through
The stone into five.
Five.

34. *Roforgell tra andsin Fintan conid*
cóir gabáil cóic cóicead hÉrend a Temraich
ocus a hUissnech, ocus conid cóir a
ngabáil-seom as cech cóiced i n-Hérind.
Celebrais iarum andsein Fintan do feraib
Hérenn isin baile sin, ocus dothóet co Dún
Tulcha i Cíarraigi Luachrai, dofánic iarum
faindi dó ocus dorigne in láidh-sea :

34 So Fintan testified afterwards that it was correct to take five provinces of Ireland from Tara and from Uisneach and that it was correct to take them from each province in Ireland. Then Fintan left the men of Ireland afterwards there in that place and he came to Dun Tulcha in Kerry of the Rushes, where afterwards weakness befell him and he made this poem:

Fand indiu mo beatha búan
romgab in críne m'imlúad.
ní clóechloim cruth armothá
is mé Fintan mac Bóchra.

Weak today is my long life
Decay has seized my motion[107]
I change shape no longer
I am Fintan son of Bochra

Bá fo dílind blíadain láin,
fo chumachta in Choimdead c[h]áid,
ocus deich cét mblíadna mbind
bá-sa am' óenur iar ndílind.

I was under the Deluge a full year
Under the power of the Holy Protector

____

[107] Literally 'has seized the decay my ability to move'

And ten-hundred harmonious years
Was I alone after the Deluge

Co tánic in dám glan glé
rogab ind nIndber Bairce,
co tucas-sa in mbé sáir sláin
Áife ingen Parrthaláin.

Then came the pure, bright company
Occupying the Inber[108] Bairce
I took as wife the very noble
Aife daughter of Partholon

Bá-sa iarsin tremsi móir
i comaimsir Parrthalóin,
co rochindsead úada amne
drong dímór bá díáirme.

I was afterwards for a long time
Contemporary with Partholon
Until there sprang from him thus
A vast throng that was innumerable

Conastánic pláig pecda
in n-oirthear Slébe Elpa,
conid dosin, dígrais gre[i]m,
atá Taimlecht ind-Hérinn.

---

[108] Inber means a rivermouth

Until came a plague of sins
From the east of the Alps[109]
From that bad weather, irresistible power,
There is Tamlecht[110] in Ireland

Tricha blíadna dam iar sin
co tángadar clann Neimid
eter Íath Boirche rop sean
ar geilt féoir cen imargal.

Thirty years afterwards I was there
Until the arrival of the children of Nemed
Between Iath Borche[111], it was ancient,
Grass grazing, without fury around

Ar Muig Ráin re flatha fiss
tucus Éblend soluscnis
siur Loga lúaithi cen fhell
ingen Chéin ocus Eithleand.

To Maige Ráin[112]before knowledge of
Heaven
I took [to wife] Eblenn of the radiant skin

---

109 Sliabh Elpa, literally the mountain of the Alps
110 Taimlecht possibly means a burial place which
would fit with this passage
111 Iath means an estate or territory. Borche is
the name of a cowherd in mythology
112 Maig Ráin = noble plain

Lugh's sister, swiftness without evil,
Daughter of Cian and Eithlenn

Is mebair lim, lúadh cech áin,
in seanchus fil ar Mag Ráin
i cath Muighi Tuiread trén
rosealgadar clanna Gomér.

The memory is with me, telling without celebration,
The poet's tradition of Maige Ráin
In the powerful battle of Maige Tuired
They slayed the children of Gomér

Bá fid fota fleascach fann
fri remis Túaithe Danann
conrucsad 'na nglúinib soir
Fomore i ndegaid Balair.

It was a long wood, abounding in pliant branches
During the time of the Tuatha De Danann
Until it was taken away east
[by] the Fomorians after Balor.

Is in drongach regda cnis
ingen Togach trethanglais
mad intan sin robo bean
anní diatá Slíab Raisen.

And the throng following after the body
Daughter of Togach[113] of the grey-stormy
sea
Because in those days in was a woman
From whom Sliab Raisen is named

Lecco ingen Tala thrén
ocus Meda mórdais géll
fosfúair is tulaig cen cheas
i farrad Meda anoirrdeas.

Lecco daughter of strong Tal
And Mid exalted by sureties
In their company on a hill without
debility
Besides Mid in the east

Ge beor indiu i nDún Tulcha
is neasa ar chách comurchra
in rí maith romalt cose
isé domrad hi faindi.

Although I am today in Dun Tulcha
Nearer and nearer to dissolution
The good King who has fostered me
It is he who has brought this weakness

---

[113] Togach literally means choice or chosen one

*35. Ronhgab tra mifrigi móir
ó'dchondairc airrdena éca do thuideacht
chuice, ocus ó rofidir corbo mithigh re Día
a bás-som do thuidecht cen clóemclodh
ndelba dó ó sin imach, conid andsen
doroindi-seom in láid-sea:*

He was seized with great dejection when
he saw the signs of death coming to him and
when he knew it was the time God had
deemed he should die without changes to his
form further from there, he then made the
following poem:

*Am crín indiu i Comor chúan
nímthá sáethar re imlúag
rogénair rogabus gre[i]m
cóecait mblíadna ría ndílind.*

I am withered today in Comor harbour
I have no trouble in telling it
I was born, I held authority
Fifty years before the Deluge

*Doridnacht dam ón ríg rél
mo sóg do thachar i cé[i]n
coic cét cóic míli cose
isé sin mét in aimsire.*

The manifest King bestowed that on me

My sufficiency he made enduring
Five hundred, five thousand hence
That is the measure of time

A Maig Mais fo díamraib de
itá Gleóir mac Glainide
is and itibis dig n-áeis
ó nach mairid dom chomáis.

In Maige Mais[114] under a mysterious haze
Where Gleoir[115] son of Glainide[116] is,
It is there I drank of age
Since none of my contemporaries remain

An cétna lonhg, líth roclas,
fúair Hérinn iar n-imarbus
is inti tánic anair
is mé mac Bóchra barrglain.

The first ship, rejoicing was heard,
Reached Ireland after the Fall
I came in it from the east
I am the son of fair-haired Bochra

Is úad rogénair ón tríath

---

114 Literally 'handsome plain'
115 Gleóir means luminous or bright
116 Made of crystal or glass, hence crystalline

ó húa Náe mac Laimiach,
iar ndíth Ceasra atú-sa trell
ic sloinded senchus Hérind.

From him I was born from the chieftain
Grandson[117] of Noah, son of Lamach
After the destruction of Cessair I have
been for a time
In telling the stories of Ireland

Is Bith mac Náe seach cech fear
cétna ránic a haitreb
ocus Ladru lúam iar sin
cétna adhnacht fo thalmain.

Bith son of Noah, distinct from every
man
The first who came to inhabit
And Ladru the steersman after that
First o be buried under the earth

Atlochar do Dia am sruith sen
don ríg rodelb ind naem-nemh
ní mo thorbond, céb eadh de
nochom chobrand mo chríne.

I give thanks to God I am an esteemed
elder

---

[117] Ua can also be read as a descendant

To the king who formed the holy heaven
Not to my advantage, whichever it is
No help is my decay to me

Cúic gabála, gním rob fearr
rogabsadar tír Hérenn
atú dia n-éisi sund seal
cosin ré-se mac Míleadh.

Five invasions, best of actions,
The taking of the land of Ireland
I have been here for a while afterwards
Until the time of the sons of Mil

Is mé Fintan, am beó búan.
is am seanchaidh sen saerslúag
nirotimart gáes ná gním glé
co romteacht áes is críne.
Am crín.

I am Fintan, I am long lived
And I am the ancient storyteller of the
noble-hosts
I was not repressed by intelligence nor
bright actions
Until I was overcome by age and decay
I am decayed.

36. Roforbastair tra Fintan a beathaid
ocus sháegul fon indus sin, ocus dofarraid

aithrighi ocus rochaith comaind ocus sacarbaigg do láim epscuip Erc meic Ochomoin meic Fidhaich, ocus dodechaid spirat Pátraic ocus Brigde co rabatar a fíadnaisi a éitsechta. Is indemin immorro cía baile in rohadhnocht, acht is dóig leo is ina chorp chollaigi rucad i nnach ndíamair ndíada amail rucad Ele ocus Enócc i pardus condafil ic ernaidi eiseiséirgi in sruthseanóir sáeghlach sin .i. Fintan mac Bóchra meic Eitheir meic Rúail meic Annida meic Caim meic Náe meic Laimiach.

There ended there Fintan's living and his period of life and ad he arrived at penance, and he consumed communion and sacrament by the hand of bishop Erc[118] son of Ochomon[119] son of Fidhaich[120], and the spirits of Patrick and Brighid came to witness his death. It is uncertain where his place of burial was, but it is likely to some that his mortal[121] body was brought to some hidden, holy place, as Elijah and Enoch

---

[118] Interestingly Erc can have a large range pf meanings including heaven, a lie, speckled red, a (red) cow, or a trout

[119] Meaning uncertain

[120] A form of fidach, meaning abounding in trees

[121] Collaigi, literally 'sinful or wicked'

were brought to Paradise, to wait the resurrection of the long-lived respected elder there, that is Fintan son of Bochra son of Ether son of Ruail son of Annid son of Ham son of Noah son of Lamech.

FINIT.
The End

Reference
Best, R. I. (1910) "The settling of the manor of Tara", Ériu 4: 121–172.